An Epistle to the Miserable

Other Titles in the Series
Letters to the Devoted Follower of Christ

Forthcoming

AN EPISTLE

TO THE MISERABLE

By

A Little Anchor of the Church

Scriptures quoted from the King James Version (KJV) of the Bible. Please note that pronouns referring to God have been capitalized, though they are not in the KJV Bible.

The Little Anchor logo is derived from an image in the public domain and it and the name Little Anchor Books have no association with any other publishing company, nor was it intended they do so. By request, this volume has been self-published.

ISBN-13: 979-8-3303-1846-9

An Epistle
to the Miserable

My dear fellow believer in Christ, grace and peace to you from God our Father and our Lord Jesus Christ, the One and Only Son of God.

We have not met, but news of your general plight reached me in a spiritual way. The Lord revealed you to me in the faces of those I have encountered. I have seen the interior agony of your soul through the eyes of others. And though I had no name for you (and very often not for them either), the heaviness and misery afflicting your soul has burdened my own heart. I see you in my mind's eye and hope I am in some measure helping you to bear up under your misery by my prayers. I see you too as I lie down at night, making it difficult to sleep.

I want to tell you a few things about when in a state of misery, and these words come directly from my own seasons of un-happiness and distress over many years. I hope your spirit is able to receive them, for I know how hard it is to receive counsel when all the soul wishes to do is

to remain feeling wretched because everything of the heavenly
feels like an affront to one's
misery. May God's Spirit aid you
in turning your face to Him.

During those times when it
seems all hope has been lost,
remind your soul of what God
has accomplished for you. If this
feels uninspiring, recall what
God has done for His own: He
saved Jacob's family alive during
famine and lifted his son Joseph
from prison to preeminence; He
rescued Israel from Egyptian
slavery—all but destroying an
entire nation to accomplish this
(though destruction would not
have been necessary if they had
let His people go as He had
commanded); He delivered His

people time and again from oppression when they cried out, even though, as it is written, "In those days there was no king in Israel: every man did that which was right in his own eyes."*

How many times did God come to His people's aid during the time of the kings? -when other nations seemingly more powerful than they came against them because they coveted the wealth and blessing of the land the LORD set aside for those who would covenant themselves to Him as a nation of priests?† And

----

* Judges 21:25—and this book makes it abundantly clear that when men did what was right in their own eyes, they easily fell into corruption.
† Exodus 19:6—"And ye shall be unto Me a kingdom of priests, and an holy nation."

though the people habitually failed to keep their side of the covenant, God chose to keep His wherever and whenever He could according to His laws which govern Man's existence.

God sent them prophets to warn, to guide, to heal, and even to raise the dead again to life. And in the fullness of time He sent His own Son to sacrifice His life for the remission of their sin and ours. All this for a stiff-necked and rebellious people who continually turned to the worship of idols than to God Almighty, El-Shaddai.* For did

---

* Genesis 17:1—"And when Abram was ninety years old and nine, the LORD appeared to Abram, and said unto him, I am the Almighty God; walk before Me, and be thou perfect."

not Moses record, "And the Lord said unto Moses, I have seen this people, and, behold, it is a stiffnecked people."[*] It is also written that the people "tempted and provoked the most high God, and kept not His testimonies: but turned back, and dealt unfaithfully like their fathers: they were turned aside like a deceitful bow."[†] But remember that it is also written: "Then they cry unto the Lord in their trouble, and He bringeth them out of their distresses."[‡] There is not time to enumerate how God came to the aid of individual persons, both in His Word and among the

---

[*] Exodus 32:9
[†] Psalm 78:56-57
[‡] Psalm 107:28

members of His people across thousands of years.

And what of your own life? It is difficult to bring His faithfulness to remembrance during such times, I know. For the soul is unruly — ever desiring to complain, to be appeased by creature comforts, and to be told the right path naturally must be the easiest one. Do not give in to the soul's self-centered demands, but you tell it to bow before the Word of the living God, the Word which is itself living and active,* in which it promises us that He is the same,

---

* Hebrews 4:12—"For the word of God is quick, and powerful, and sharper than any twoedged sword, piercing even to the dividing asunder of soul and spirit, and of the joints and marrow, and is a discerner of the thoughts and intents of the heart."

His years shall have no end, and
the children of His servants shall
continue — that means, *not*
destroyed — and their seed shall
be established before Him.*

So put on the full armor of God,
thou mighty spiritual soldier of
valor, as the angel of the LORD
told cowering and hopeless
Gideon,† not forgetting the shoes
of the gospel of peace,‡ which the
enemy has not the power to
remove from your feet. It is, as

---

* Psalm 102:27-28
† Judges 6:12—"And the angel of the LORD
appeared unto him, and said unto him,
The LORD is with thee, thou mighty man
of valour."
‡ Ephesians 6:15—"And your feet shod
with the preparation of the gospel of
peace."

our Lord declared, "Peace [O my soul] I leave with you"; and our Lord never lied to us or constantly fed us disinformation (and no matter how necessary a bit might be now and again to an enemy who lies to us with every breath, I daresay the freedom to make use of it has been abused of late in this great war of good against evil). "My peace I give unto you," He told us, "not as the world giveth, give I unto you."* Nothing earthly or demonic has the power or authority to take away what He promised to us if we are unwilling to relinquish it. The enemy hovers to see if we will casually set aside God's

---

* John 14:27

words rather than hold fast to them, like a thief eyeing your wallet on a store counter who will grab what you let go of the instant he has opportunity to take it. Don't give him the opportunity to steal from you.

Remember too that our Lord did not come to bring peace to those who love the things of this earth more than they love Him.[*] And the enemies of God desire to bring us unto destruction—

---

[*] Matthew 10:34, 37-39—"Think not that I am come to send peace on earth: I came not to send peace, but a sword....He that loveth father or mother more than Me is not worthy of Me: and he that loveth son or daughter more than Me is not worthy of Me. And he that taketh not his cross, and followeth after Me, is not worthy of Me. He that findeth his life shall lose it: and he that loseth his life for My sake shall find it."

whether or not they win or lose. On the cusp of losing, they are even more ferocious against those who are marked by the Blood of Jesus of Nazareth. So we must recall with reason that peace is always ours by right of promise, but there is an enemy on the prowl who continually seeks to steal it from us.*

As difficult as life is for you at times, as onerously hard as it is to find something for which to be grateful, do not declare that God has not helped you. If you cannot

---

* I Peter 5:8—"Be sober, be vigilant; because your adversary the devil, as a roaring lion, walketh about, seeking whom he may devour"; John 10:10—"The thief cometh not, but for to steal, and to kill, and to destroy: I am come that they might have life, and that they might have it more abundantly."

say something excellent and worthy of being spoken, say nothing at all. Do not let your soul get away with saying—even alone to yourself when you can help it—that God has done nothing for you. Correct yourself as is fitting of one who has been accorded a high, heavenly seat in Christ "even when we were dead in sins, hath quickened us together with Christ…and hath raised us up together, and made us sit together in heavenly places in Christ Jesus."* Remember that it is by grace we are saved; "we have redemption through His blood, the forgiveness of sins, ac-

---

cording to the riches of His grace."*

We can never stand before God and declare that someone has wronged us based on the merit of our own innocence. We may certainly be innocent of the crimes for which the enemy is trying to bring us to account, but as we all stand guilty of sins before God, no soul can say that it is better than the one standing next to it. No soul can confidently declare that it is unstained of sin while the one accusing it is not. Your sin, though it may be far removed from the accusations made against you, still exists but for the Blood of Christ. There was

<hr>

* Ephesians 1:7

and is nothing you could do to lessen or erase it. Therefore, before the Great High Bench of the Most High Judge of the universe, apart from this grace of the atoning Blood, you *do* stand guilty of crimes against God and humanity. So do not be tempted to get up on a high horse and proclaim your innocence. Be humble. Be teachable. Remember Job.

When you feel fractious, disgruntled, or argumentative, or you are tempted to grumbling despair, take yourself as quickly as you can—even if you are able only in the inner man—into your prayer cell and fall on your knees. If you cannot immediately repent for your ungracious attitude for all the Lord has done, is doing, and will do for you all the rest of your life, give voice to your grievances as Elijah did on Sinai. He was honest about what was oppressing his soul, but he did not declare that God had not done right by him.* But be careful that such grievances are for God's ears alone during such moments, because Man's heart is frail. It cannot often bear to hear such struggles voiced and keep all the while its own weak faith. If you have any love for your fellow souls at all, you will spare them your undisciplined moment of venting until you are past it and the Lord has called you later to

---

* I Kings 19

incorporate it somehow into your testimony. Was not Elijah's hard time incorporated later into Scripture? But we have no reason to believe by what we have been given in I Kings 19 that he immediately told his new protégé Elisha all that had just passed between God and himself.

Do not be tempted to think so much of your own misery that you place a higher value on giving voice to it than on the faith of your fellow souls—for God declares the value of their faith is "much more precious than of gold that perisheth."* Should a heart that has so long journeyed with God be so frail? No, of

---

* I Peter 1:7

course not. But the theoretical state is often far from the practical state of things.

When you are finished with your grievances, do not rise from your knees or your spiritual place of humble repentance, without first uttering a little praise to God for what He has done for you, even if the only thing for which you can think to thank Him is far in the past and you have already thanked Him for this on numerous occasions. Sincere gratitude for what He has done for us never returns void.* And exer-

---

* Isaiah 55:11—"So shall My word be that goeth forth out of My mouth: it shall not return unto Me void, but it shall accomplish that which I please, and it shall prosper in the thing whereto I sent it." Recall that John 1:1 teaches us that Jesus Christ is the very incarnation of

cise a little faith in thanking Him for what He is about to do for you. Your heart may not believe this, but command your soul anyway to obey your injunction to state this or to keep from uttering grumblings. Do not let your soul command your spirit in such matters or you will quickly lose the high ground you fought so valiantly to obtain in the journey of your Christ-life.

And I tell you the truth, doubting not an iota in my faith that this is indeed the truth of the matter: to conquer your soul — the heart, will, mind, and emotions — in what appears to be

---

God's powerful Word that goes forth from His being and His will. Consider the importance of our words as those made in God's image.

a small spiritual act as this one, is from God's perspective one of the greatest victories a soldier of Christ can achieve. Man tells us great warriors undergo great physical challenges to achieve great victories, but the Lord told us that it is the poor in spirit who gain a whole heavenly realm,* and it is the humble who will inherit this earth.† When we wage spiritual war, we fight with spiritual weapons, not carnal ones‡; and it is when we most feel our

---

* Matthew 5:3—"Blessed are the poor in spirit: for theirs is the kingdom of heaven."
† Matthew 5:5—"Blessed are the meek: for they shall inherit the earth."
‡ II Corinthians 10:4—"For the weapons of our warfare are not carnal, but mighty through God to the pulling down of strong holds."

misery, when we most want to let weak arms drop, that God is poised to reckon reward in His accounting books to the soul who courageously utters a few words in faith when the soul can see no way out of its misery.

Recall to your soul too that faith is not feeling. Our poor heart, weak in faith, may not feel the Lord's presence. It may not feel that its prayers have been heard — or heard in a way worthy of being answered. It may not feel that anything has changed by its simple declaration of praise and gratitude and repentance. It may not feel terribly spiritual or even particularly repentant (and we know it does not feel grateful or inclined to praise in its natural, unruly state). Even so, a soul performs these small acts of obeisance to God because it chooses to believe His Word, which teaches us such an attitude toward Him is right and pleasing. "Enter into His gates with thanksgiving, and into His courts with praise: be thankful unto Him, and bless His name."* "But without faith it is impossible to please Him: for he that cometh to God must believe that He is, and that He is a rewarder of them that diligently seek Him."†

Certainly you believe that He is, that He is the Lord, Yahweh the Self-Existent One — whether

---

* Psalm 100:4
† Hebrews 11:6

or not you were able to express yourself coherently like this about Him—or you would not have bothered to bring your grievances to Him in the first place. On some level you prayed because you believe that He is GOD and you are not. So there is fully half of the promise's conditions met right there. Now all your soul has to do is to stir itself up to believe God is also One Who Rewards those souls who seek Him. And did you not just do that also? -seek Him out? Who were you speaking to in your misery? -your fairy godmother? -the coworker who noticed you talking seemingly to yourself? How often is a soul stopped in its progression right here, in that place before the signpost which directs belief in the Rewarder?

Forget what you have been taught. Many teachers did not mean to deceive, but we can hardly expect those to be free from error who were themselves deceived by erroneous teaching. Forgive and forget. For have you not also committed many sins that require others to apply toward you the principle of forgiving and forgetting? Forgive, forget, and move on. Accept the Word as it is and what it tells you. It tells us that God is a Rewarder. Will the God who is love reward you with more misery?* Heaven forbid! There is no misery in Heaven, and the Lord Himself taught us to pray that as life is in Heaven, so should it be on this earth.† Moreover, His Word teaches us that "the blessing of the LORD, it maketh rich, *and He addeth no sorrow with it.*"‡

Faith is not dictated to by feeling. If feeling does dictate to it, then there is no faith being exercised. It is all feeling. You can *feel* and still have faith. But you cannot let feeling dictate to your

---

* I John 4:16—"And we have known and believed the love that God hath to us. God is love; and he that dwelleth in love dwelleth in God, and God in him."

† Luke 11:2—"And He said unto them, When ye pray, say, Our Father which art in heaven, Hallowed be Thy name. Thy kingdom come. Thy will be done, as in heaven, so in earth."

‡ Proverbs 10:22, emphasis added.

faith and have that faith remain untransformed by it. To be miserable is to feel misery. Do not let the misery you feel dictate to your soul when you strive to exercise your faith. Neither ought the spirit be dictated to by the soul, for true faith—that reborn-in-Christ living relationship with a Person who is trustworthy of our faith—is of the spirit. We can stand up to those who have chosen to be God's enemies. But often we need to stand up to our own soul and tell it what for. It is very often our own soul that needs a good upper cut on its spiritual jaw than our war with the enemy needs fought with physical weapons of fists and fury. Being triggered to feel misery often comes upon us from outside. But remaining in a state of misery generally is a matter of soul.

Recall to your soul as often as needs be that God is mindful of our misery. Does it not say in His Word that He is so? "And the LORD said, I have surely seen the affliction of My people which are in Egypt, and have heard their cry by reason of their task-masters; for I know their sorrows."* "And they put away the strange gods from among them, and served the LORD: and His soul was grieved for the misery of Israel."† And does not Scripture teach us that misery is

---

* Exodus 3:7
† Judges 10:16

sometimes permitted by God to turn us to Him so that He may turn our plight (especially when we needed correcting)? "I will go and return to My place, till they acknowledge their offence, and seek My face: in their affliction they will seek Me early."* The next verses declare the people's response: "Come, and let us return unto the LORD: for He hath torn, and He will heal us; He hath smitten, and He will bind us up. After two days will He revive us: in the third day He will raise us up, and we shall live in His sight. Then shall we know, if we follow on to know the LORD: His going forth is prepared as the morning;

---

* Hosea 5:15

and He shall come unto us as the
rain, as the latter and former rain
unto the earth."*

---

* Hosea 6:1-3. The first correlation of three
days is obviously that Christ was
resurrected on the third day, thus
enabling us in Him to live the resurrected
life, which is to be raised up from the
curse of death and all its manifestations
in our life. One can also consider that two
days' worth of sincere repentance is
required to be then lifted up to a life lived
in His light, under the banner of divine
favor. It takes time to return to God—not
because He needs more than an instant to
change things, but because the soul is so
unruly. We accomplish nothing if we do
not in our spirit rise up and take
authority over our soul and commit or
recommit ourself to the Christ-life. And
thirdly, consider that a thousand years is
as one day to God (II Peter 3:8); therefore
consider that two days (two thousand
years) have passed since God made
Himself manifest to us and then left again
(i.e., ascended to Heaven). So it is worth
considering that, according to this
paradigm, during this third millennium
since the first Advent of Christ, the

Did He write these things for His benefit? Not at all! Is it not also written that the Lord Himself said, "Can a woman forget her sucking child, that she should not have compassion on the son of her womb? yea, they may forget, yet will I not forget thee. Behold, I have graven thee upon the palms of My hands; thy walls are continually before Me."* He never forgets us. He perpetually bears on Himself the marks of the lengths to which He went to restore us to Himself. It is we who forget, and often very easily. If you doubt this, read Matthew 13:19-23 and humbly

---

consider how often the Seed of Christ (His teachings, His sacrificial nature, His atoning life and redemptive blood, etc.) falls into good soil in your soul. We *must* cease, if we are ever to become that Bride without spot or wrinkle,* to cry out with every new trial that we have given enough and are now entitled to take ourself to the sofa to eat to excess and to be distracted by electronic boxes. Yet always remember that God is also the Healer,† and it is an easy thing for Him to transform the earth of your soul into good soil that can birth good harvests of many crops. He only requires your

---

* Ephesians 5:27
† Exodus 15:26

willingness, your *sincere and committed* willingness, before accomplishing it, which requires more than half an hour of good intentions. If this willingness does not survive a good meal and a night's sleep, it was not real.

Are we stupid or what? (Perhaps I should write you a separate letter on the subject of the natural stupidity of Man, if this would be profitable to your soul.) The Sinless One who permitted Himself to be scourged and nailed to a cross until the labor of the remission of our sin should be finished does not—*cannot*—look upon our misery with an unfeeling heart. You, especially in the small exercises of your faith when to render them is the most difficult, are as the apple of His eye.* You in a sense are the treasure hidden in a field the Son of Man sold all He had in this earth so that He could buy your citizenship (and your very life) for His Father's Kingdom.†

Soon after giving this parable to His disciples, Jesus asked them, "Have ye understood all these things?"‡ They answered Him yes. If you have understood His teachings to you, live them.

---

* Deuteronomy 32:10—"He found him [Israel] in a desert land, and in the waste howling wilderness; He led him about, He instructed him, He kept him as the apple of His eye."

† Matthew 13:44—"Again, the kingdom of heaven is like unto treasure hid in a field; the which when a man hath found, he hideth, and for joy thereof goeth and selleth all that he hath, and buyeth that field."

‡ Matthew 13:51

You may feel miserable, but tell your unruly heart that its misery will not dictate how you will live before God. If all you can wrench from that stiff-necked soul of yours is one moment of bended knee or a few words of gratitude uttered in faith unadorned by feeling (even the feeling of any love for God in that moment), I guarantee you: God *will* hear your cries of misery, and He WILL come to your rescue. We plant the seed of faith, but God brings it unto a great harvest.* Do not dig up the seeds to see how they are doing, but leave them under the dark soil of your soul for the Holy Spirit to cultivate as God wills. In

---

* Mark 4:26-29; I Corinthians 3:6-7

His timing the tide will turn; and in the meantime, your misery will abate. In truth, it often abates in that very moment the soul threw itself at God's feet. The overall life struggle does not always immediately pass, but by His grace the misery does. And in this time, there is often much resolution for difficulties. Why? *Because He heard your cries of misery and answered your prayers.*

If you feel nothing as you read these words, that is all right: for feeling, remember, has no lawful authority over faith; and faith, true faith, has no spiritual bond with feeling. Fact stands between them: there is too great a disparity between faith and feeling. It is like a tremendous valley, like a crevasse in a mountain range, dividing them. I tell you the truth, it is better to throw yourself off the precipice of feeling into the crevasse of fact, which is the Word of God and all His precious promises to us, than to remain and never find a way to cross that void. You will not be harmed — or not irreparably — by casting yourself off the precipice of feeling. And once in that deep valley, turn your back upon feeling and begin the search for that almost imperceptible path up the mountain of faith. I guarantee you, it is there. And I guarantee you, you will not lose your feeling for God and your fellow souls; all you will have done is to turn your back on the philosophy that feeling is a mountain worth living on. There is much better and more fruitful land on the mountain of faith, I assure you. Get your house in order for a great move.

Please receive these words of encouragement, meant kindly, and then wait on God for a bountiful harvest which is the release from misery. Hold fast to God, the trustworthy Person, during those moments when it is difficult to recall any of His specific words, and let Him bear the burden of your life.

Farewell—FARE WELL, I declare unto your soul in Jesus' mighty Name. I hope with all my heart that your misery would quickly pass away, that the light of Christ would eclipse that tormenting darkness, that you would be able to feel the joy of the LORD which is our strength.*

The grace of our Lord Jesus Christ, the love of the Father, and the fellowship of the Holy Spirit be with you always. Amen.

---

* Nehemiah 8:10